FORT KLAMATH

FRONTIER POST IN OREGON

1863-1890

BUENA COBB STONE

979.4

Royal Publishing Company

General Book Publishers
7918 Maxwell, Dallas, Texas 75217

DEDICATION

This book is dedicated to all who love the Klamath Basin; the moonlight shimmering on her lakes; the blue and violet shadows that drape her hills; her crisp and sunny days; the cinnamon bark of her stately Ponderosa pines; the waterfowl in flight patterns against her blue skies; and most of all the friendly folks who make her what she is.

ACKNOWLEDGEMENTS

J. Neilson Barry (deceased)—Oregon historian who started me on this book, and furnished material and a great deal of encouragement.

Colonel Harry C. Larter Jr. (deceased)—who answered in detail many questions about the Army, with enthusiasm and with many little sketches.

Heirs of Orson A. Stearns, soldier at Fort Klamath, who furnished reminiscences and letters of great value.

Priscilla Knuth, Oregon Historical Society, who gave full co-operation in making available the Society's documents and photographs.

Thelma E. Bedell, Chief, Reader's Service Division of the Library at the United States Military Academy at West Point, who checked about the branding of deserters.

Company of Military Collectors and Historians who put me in touch with Colonel Larter and others who were helpful.

The Loosley family for memoirs about Fort Klamath.

Klamath County Museum for data and some photographs.

Numerous old-timers of the Klamath Country who remembered the fort.

Harold Ashley, Fort Klamath buff, for picture selection and arrangement.

Lowell Kaup to whom I am indebted for continuing encouragement and support.

Francis Landrum, engineer and history enthusiast, who produced the accompanying maps for this book.

FOREWORD

This is a simple story of men who did their duty in critical days. It could have been a much longer and documented volume, but this serves my purpose better. In no sense is it to be considered a history of the Modoc Indian War, save in the effect of that war on the men who were compelled to hunt their elusive foe at a time when the President and the Secretary of War, though themselves military men, underestimated the situation and needs of the soldiers.

This account is written in the hope that we shall never forget the soldiers who made their bivouacs amid the sage and sand or in snow and sleet; who daily put their lives in jeopardy, unsung and underpaid—often short of food and water; paying with their lives for others' blunders.

The glory of the cavalry is a departed glory, but in the period covered in this story, they carried on their proud tradition and served at great sacrifices, and over incredible distances.

Let these words, then, be a tribute to the soldiers who manned the far-flung frontier posts of the West.

CONTENTS

Part I

CIVILIANS INTO SOLDIERS

The country was engaged in a fratricidal war. The army had called most of the regular soldiers to the scene of the conflict, leaving the West exposed to Indian uprisings and internal strife.

The state legislature of Oregon asked Congress for additional military posts, including one at the Klamath Lakes, and for the removal of the Indians to reservations where they could be controlled more easily. They were a constant source of danger to immigrants and settlers alike. The other need for troops was the divided loyalty of citizens. Many Confederate sympathizers lived on the Pacific Coast, and there was even an attempt to organize a Pacific Republic, loyal to neither side. These sympathizers were organized into the Knights of the Golden Circle, and were said to drill at night and were even suspected of overt acts.

Under authority of the War Department, Colonel George Wright, in charge of the Northwest, appointed Thomas R. Cornelius as colonel; Reuben F. Maury as lieutenant colonel; Benjamin F. Harding as quartermaster; C. S. Drew and J. S. Rinearson as majors. He authorized them to recruit a cavalry for volunteer service in Oregon, with a minimum of sixty-four in each company, and a maximum of eighty-two.

9

The following is a copy of the recruiting poster they had issued:

CAVALRY! CAVALRY!
RALLY VOLUNTEERS!

to the United States Service for Frontier Protection.
Term of service 3 years unless sooner discharged.
Each man will be required to furnish his own horse and horse equipment. The total amount of pay per month for man and horse will be—

> 1st Sgt. $39
> Other Sgts. $36
> Corporals $33
> Blacksmiths and farriers $34
> Buglers $32
> Privates $31

Clothing and arms furnished the men same as in the regular army, and $100 bounty at the expiration of services.

AN ENROLLING OFFICE

for enlistment of volunteers has been opened at Jacksonville and other officers will be established at points in Josephine and Douglas counties as soon as practicable.

R. F. Maury
Lt. Col. O. C. R.

Jacksonville, November 21, 1861

With the new gold mines opened in Idaho, plenty of good work at fair wages, the prospect of patrol duty along the frontier and border Indian fighting instead of the glory of battlefields, there was little inducement for young men to enlist. Those who did so were inspired by patriotic duty. They left pleasant homes and profitable occupations to take up arms in defense of the frontier against Indian attacks and against attempts to dissolve the Union. It is pleasant to report that they had a far better record of performing duties than most of the regular army regiments. Most of them were sober young fellows from the farms of Oregon, and they came in singing this ditty:

> I'm a raw recruit with a brand new suit.
> One hundred dollars bounty,
> And I've just come down to Ashland town,
> To fight for Jackson County.

The First Oregon Cavalry patrolled the overland trail, and served as scouts and escorts. They covered thousands of miles. Besides the exceptional hardships they endured, the cavalrymen suffered by the repeal by Congress of the Act of 1861 which had allowed forty cents per day for horse forage. Their personal mounts became thin from hard work. Often the cavalry troops had to lay down their rifles and perform hard work with axes and shovels as they cleared the road for wagons, escorted immigrant trains, and pursued Indians or renegades who preyed on the settlers.

The need for military protection in the Klamath country was obvious. Along the Southern Route of the Oregon Trail, there had been bloody massacres, so the region of the Lost River Gap was considered for a military post. Another site considered was on the hills where the town of Klamath Falls is now located. The third was in the Wood River Valley, near Upper Klamath Lake, and that site was chosen.

In March 1863, Major C. S. Drew, at Camp Baker in Jackson County, received orders from the Department of the Pacific to make a reconnaissance as far east as the Owyhee. After completing this survey, he made his decision. He chose the Wood River Valley because the lush grass would provide ample feed for cavalry horses and mules; because the six streams of crystal water would furnish ample supplies for all needs; because the beautiful forests of pine would supply needed timber and fuel; and because the location was near several trails—the old Nez Perce, the Rogue Valley to eastern Oregon mines, and the new Oregon Central Military Road.

The location was 42 degrees north latitude and 121 degrees west longitude. The Wood River Valley floor is six to fifteen miles wide, and it lies between mountains, hence its Indian name of "i-ukah." On the west are the forested Cascades; Sun Mountain is on the north; on the east lies a ridge some 400 to 600 feet in height. This the Indians called Sullix, meaning mad, probably because of the deep-throated echo given back by the cliff. To the south, the country opens up, onto the Klamath Basin, with Mount Shasta looming grandly in the distance, sometimes all pale and ethereal, sometimes with the rosy light of the alpen-glow making it a flaming jewel. The valley seems hedged about with mountains and undulating ridges; it was a waving wilderness of grass, with infinite distances and untrammeled domains, when Drew selected the spot. Later, when surveys were made it was found that the post was in Township 33 South, Range 7½ East, Willamette Meridian.

The disadvantages of the location were that it was too far away from the Southern Route to furnish help to immigrants; and too far away from the turbulent Modoc Indians, as was later shown. However, the site was approved by Captain Robert S. Williamson who had explored through the Klamath region in 1855, and by Brigadier-General Benjamin Alvord, in command of the Department of Oregon, 1861-1865.

Complaints of political favoritism in the choice persisted, and so the Department of the Pacific in San Francisco, sent Captain James Van Voast to inspect the site and buildings under way, in November, 1863. He reported that the adverse reports seemed to have emanated from a disgruntled sub-agent of the Indian Department. Van Voast reported, "There can be no question of the fitness of the place selected for the new fort if the only considerations are the health of the troops and the concern for their support. It also appears equally clear that as a strategic position taken for the purpose of holding in subjection the Indians that are considered hostile, it offers many advantages. Indeed, with the limited means at Colonel Drew's disposal for the construction of the new fort in that section of the country, it is hardly possible that one could have been located which would have afforded greater advantage and secured like protection to emigrants and to citizens . . . Citizens understand little with regard to the mode of supplying troops; therefore transactions which in themselves are proper and which save the Government much unnecessary expense, excite their suspicion, and call forth from them remarks which have not the slightest foundation in reason or fact. And this is the more especially the case when a person whose political faith is a question with a portion of the community is in any way engaged in supplying troops . . . "

The fort was eight miles north of Upper Klamath Lake, lying in the southern part of Wood River Valley. Its location was in the most pleasant and beautiful part, with a southern exposure.

Captain William Kelly and C Troop of the First Oregon Volunteer Cavalry was sent to construct and garrison the post as planned by Colonel Drew. David Linn, of Jacksonville, was the civilian contractor. A primitive sawmill was installed on Fort Creek, then called Linn Creek, which prepared lumber for the buildings. The structures erected that year, and which served until regulars garrisoned the post, were nearly all built of box lumber, though some few were of logs. There were quarters for four officers; an adjutant's office; a guard house and an arsenal; storehouses for the quartermaster and commissary supplies; a small hospital and a company bakery. Barracks for the two companies were in a long double building, with two small additions for first sergeants' offices.

The stables for horses of the two troops were the best and most substantial of all the buildings, according to the men, who said that the horses fared better than they. So they could well sing the Stable Call:

O go to the stable as soon as you're able,
Water your horses and give them some corn;
For if you don't do it the colonel will know it,
And then you will rue it as sure as you're born.

In the center of the parade ground, the flag pole was erected. This pole of 125 feet was not only the symbol of government in this far outpost, but it was the center from which all surveying and measuring

14

was done for the military and hay reserves. The high-flying flag was the first thing seen by travelers.

The military reserve contained 1,050.24 acres, while to the north, was the hay reserve of 3,135 acres. There the lush grass for which the valley is famous, provided hay in abundance. At first the cutting was done by soldiers, but at a later date hay contracts were made, at four or five dollars per ton.

The troops not only garrisoned the fort, but they were also called on to aid the Indian Agent at the Klamath Reservation five miles to the south. They had hardly arrived at their station, when called upon to capture a suspected murderer. Skookum John, a Klamath war chief, was killed in November, 1863, by the officers, while they were trying to arrest him for murders committed on the Rancheria Prairie. From the post the cavalry went out on long reconnaissances, and on forays against the hostiles. Other posts were established at Fort Bidwell, in the northeast corner of California, and at Camp Harney and Camp Warner in eastern Oregon.

The soldiers were also road-builers. The first road from Jacksonville, the supply point, was begun at once upon their arrival. It was known as the Rancheria Trail, because it ran along Rancheria Prairie and north of Mt. McLoughlin. It was rough and precipitous from the Prairie on Butte Creek, but over it they dragged the sawmill machinery, past Four-Mile Lake and other lakes, to Klamath Lake where Harrison Lodge now is, thence along the lake to Seven-Mile Creek and across Wood River to the post.

The most important event of 1864 was the gathering of the tribes at Council Grove for a treaty with the United States. Klamaths, Modocs, and Yahooskin Snakes were represented by the chief men. There, in

October, 1864, the tribes agreed to relinquish their lands and go on the Klamath Reservation in exchange for specified rights and annuities.

In 1865, Company I, Oregon Volunteer Infantry was added to Fort Klamath. The company had been recruited in Jackson County, so they knew the country. In later years, some of the men were to remember with nostalgia, how they mustered at Camp Baker, with ceremonies that included a flag presentation and speeches; their march across the Cascade Mountains to Fort Klamath; how they killed an elk en route and one hungry recruit sat up most of the night roasting choice bits; how they diverted a small creek and feasted on the great catch of fish; how they were met at Williamson River ford by a detachment of cavalry who escorted them to the post, where they were officially welcomed by Captain Kelly and staff.

That summer, Captain Sprague and a mulatto, John Matthews, a pioneer frontiersman, selected a route for a new road. Then twenty men of Company I were assigned to open the road. The new route was from Union Creek on the Rogue River, across the mountains, down along the ridge by the canyon now called Annie Creek, and on to the post. This was very much the route used today. It was while on this work of road-building that the men came across the famous Crater Lake. They were the first men to climb down to its deep blue waters of mystery and unapproachable majesty. Captain Sprague named it Lake Majesty, and then wrote a description for the newspaper, the first printed description of that now world-famous wonder.

Life was arduous, but not monotonous. The country abounded in game. Bear, deer and antelope could be found in sight of the fort. Ducks and geese and other water fowl by the millions came along the Pacific Flyway to nest in the reedy shores. In the many streams were salmon trout up to fifteen pounds in size, and from the Indians the soldiers learned how to spear fish through the ice in winter. But loneliness was a problem, for they were very isolated. The fort was thirty-six miles from Linkville, (now Klamath Falls); ninety-eight from Jacksonville; one hundred twenty-five from Ashland; and even one hundred thirty miles from the nearest military post, Camp Warner.

Civilian employees were common, and their names are not of interest save that of George Neuse (later spelled Nurse) who was employed at the post in the summer of 1865. He and his wagon and four-mule team were employed to remove the down timber and other obstructions on the Rancheria Trail, at $8 per day. Soon after, he became the sutler at the post, very much aware of shipping needs. By 1867, he was to establish a ferry where Link River was crossed, and thus was the founder of Linkville, which was to grow into the city of Klamath Falls on Link River, which short stream is entirely within the city limits today.

An expedition was formed and fitted out to go to the Steens Mountains country to establish a winter camp and break up the camp of Snake Indians there. They built a bridge of tules at Lake Warner and had to pull the wagons by hand because the horses mired down. They camped in their wet clothes. There they constructed a temporary post, Camp Alford. They had to go to the mountains to get juniper logs, often leaving their guns at camp, a mile away. When this task was finished, a detachment was ordered back to Fort Klamath. The trip was most disagreeable, for they were some two weeks enroute, with snow or rain their daily companion. They arrived at the fort in the midst of a snow storm. They were bone weary and chilled to the marrow when they reached quarters that cold November day in 1865. Young men, scarcely out of their teens, they were also ravenous. This fact led to rather serious consequences.

All winter fare had been poor. To add to their problem, the commander and quartermaster received the flour ration and hired a baker. If the men wanted more bread than was served them, they could buy it at 12 and a half cents per pound. Many of the young men spent half their wages for dry bread. There were no commissionary purchases and the sutler had only whiskey, cards, and tobacco; no fruit or vegetables were on hand.

As for the garrison supplies, there were "dessicated potatoes" which resembled cornmeal; "mixed vegetables" which came in squares and were packed in five-gallon cans. The squares were two inches thick and resembled leaf tobacco. A four-inch square would swell to fill a five-gallon kettle, when the cabbage leaves, tomatoes, carrots, turnips and pumpkin vines became clearly visible. This was sometimes mixed with sow-belly to make a soup which the men dubbed "nitro-glycerin soup" because it was so strong. *Breakfast* usually consisted of six ounces of bread, frozen; a small piece of beefsteak, frozen; and coffee hot and black. *Dinner* at noon was the grand meal. The menu might be soup, beans or rice or mixed vegetables, boiled beef or pork, and coffee. *Supper* was left-over meat, bread and coffee. Considering the hard work of cutting and hauling wood for all the buildings, shoveling snow, cutting and stacking hay, cleaning the stables, this was mighty poor fare for hungry men.

So on that November 25th, sixty wet and hungry men came in from having built Camp Alford. They had

had hard travel, being without tents; had had their scanty commissary supplies raided by Indian dogs at Sprague River Narrows. They were given their flour ration, but instead of delivering it to the bakery as ordered to do, they took it to their messhouse, prepared to have a feast of pancakes. They were arrested and ordered individually to turn the flour to the bakery. At first they refused, and then complied. The first man to refuse was sixteen-year-old Fullerton. As punishment, he was strung up by his thumbs to a tamarack bush, with his toes just touching the ground to support his weight. By night, as the snow fell heavier, a rattle of hammers in company headquarters indicated a loading of muskets, but Fullerton was returned to the guardhouse before the men could act. There was standing room only in the guardhouse that night, as sixty-five men were crowded into the room. The major read a few selections from the Articles of War, and told the men they had committed an offense subject to courtmartial for which the penalty might be death. He had decided to free them, however, "because the war is over." Thus ended what was known as the Bread Riot. It is pleasant to report that the young man so cruelly punished, was later to become a leading lawyer, circuit judge and state senator.

There was tragedy, too, at the post. The first day of April, 1866, was heralded by the mellow notes of the bugle, awakening the slumbering garrison to the usual routine of roll call, breakfast, sick call, guard mount, and the adjutant's call. The day was one of those cold days of early spring, when the ground was nearly destitute of its snow covering, but still retained the frosts of winter, and pools of water filled the depressions. The mountains and timbered portions of the valley were still under varying depths of snow, that some weeks earlier had reached more than four feet on the level. The sun seemed to have no warmth, as though it, too, felt the chill of frost.

Those of the garrison who were not on guard or police duty, were generally engaged in some indoor games, for the ground was too damp for outdoor exercise and games. Some little excitement had been created a few days earlier by the return of five men of Company I from furlough that had been spent in Rogue River Valley, they crossed the mountains by Rancheria Trail on the frozen crust of the snow. There had been six when the party left, but only five returned.

Stephen T. Hallock, one of the most respected members of the company, a man of deep religious feeling and sterling honor, had undertaken the trip to arrange some business affairs that he had left to enter the army at his country's call, had failed to meet his fellows at the point agreed upon from which to start back to the post. As the weather was threatening, his comrades were afraid to delay their start, and, thinking he would overtake them on the road, pushed on. They accomplished their more than ninety miles without serious trouble, though the snow was becoming very rotten during the middle of the day, so that they were compelled to travel early and late to get over it.

No one believed that Hallock had deserted, or thought he would fail to report by the expiration of his leave; but when the morning's report of his company showed him "absent without leave," and day after day passed until his name was dropped, and he was registered as a deserter, there was genuine sorrow among his comrades.

Just after the noon meal on this April 1st, one of the boys decided he would go fishing in Wood River. He followed the road toward the old pole bridge, and was astonished to discover some object resembling a human being lying partly in a pool of water and partly on one of the projecting stringers. A near approach disclosed the fact that the object was a soldier, and that soldier was Stephen T. Hallock—not dead, but so nearly so that he was unconscious. His clothing was muddy and frozen, and his features blue and swollen.

Securing help, they took the poor fellow to the hospital where every effort was made during the afternoon and until early next morning to restore vitality to the shivering form. He was rubbed with snow by warm hands, was chaffed with brandy and wrapped in warm blankets, but no reaction from the terrible chill was evident. Before the bugle sounded for reveille on April 2nd, taps had sounded for Private Stephen T. Hallock.

In order to learn the true story of their comrade's delay and exposure, some of his friends took up the back trail and followed it for twelve miles. The facts they learned from the examination and those learned later, revealed one of the most remarkable cases of physical endurance and devotion to duty that is on record.

It seems that Hallock had been delayed in his start by business, and did not leave until the day after his comrades. Soon after reaching the snow, which began at Rancheria Prairie, some fifty miles from the fort, a rain storm came up. Being a short man and encumbered with his blankets and provisions, his progress through the snow was slow, and he was several days covering the same distance that his comrades had made in one day. There was every reason to believe that he had spent several nights without fire or shelter other than the overhanging boughs; that, knowing his furlough had expired, he struggled along day and night.

He evidently reached Seven-Mile Creek in the evening of March 31st, and in attempting to cross the foot-log, had slipped off into the icy water, as his blankets and knapsack (the latter empty) were found hanging on a stump near where he emerged from the water. From that creek he wandered up along the valley, evidently unable to see the way, until he struck the road from Crater Lake and Annie Creek. Here the water from melting snow had run down the wagon tracks, leaving a black mark which he had been able to follow. He had staggered badly, and frequently had fallen exhausted, only to rise again and struggle on. His falls were more frequent, until within a mile and a half of the bridge, he had begun to crawl. Here he evidently fixed his Colt revolver, as powder was scattered on the snow where he had fallen. His revolver was found with one barrel discharged in his vain attempt to attract attenion, and the caps snapped on the other five barrels showed that he had exhausted every means at hand. From this point to where he was found, in sight and sound of the post, he had crawled slowly and painfully for a mile and a half before sinking into unconsciousness from overexertion and exposure.

Undoubtedly he heard the bugle for reveille. One of the sentries on post had heard a shot fired in the early morning, but remembered it was April 1st and thought someone was trying to fool him, so did not report it to the sergeant of the guard. Had that shot been reported, the life of a brave man might have been saved.

Today he rests at the Presidio Cemetery in San Francisco, where the bodies were taken when the post was abandoned. Private Stephen T. Hallock rests in the west section, in grave No. 465.

Although the war between the states ended in 1865, Company I, 1st Oregon Volunteer Infantry, found itself still on duty at Fort Klamath in the winter of 1866-67. Lack of transportation and great distances from the East; the gigantic tasks of reconstruction; the filling of important posts with regulars to replace volunteers were some of the reasons given for their retention. The fact remains that this company was one of the last to be mustered out in all the country.

Captain F. B. Sprague commanded the post, and saw to it that the duties were not rigid or onerous. The garrison spent most of its time in chores and in guard duties, so they had plenty of time to fret about getting home. Sprague had abolished the selling of bread; had used post funds for the purchase of dried fruits and vegetables; had used the quartermaster teams to bring in food from the Rogue Valley, so the post was fairly well supplied with a variety of food. Moreover, in the spring of 1867, Oliver C. Applegate, with twenty Indians, had opened a road from The Dalles, and supplies could come in by that route.

Of books and periodicals the men had none except copies of the Jacksonville papers and a few copies of fiction owned by the men. So, to relieve the monotony and provide some measure of entertainment, they started a weekly newspaper of their own, appropriately named *The Growler*. Orson A. Stearns was the editor. Having no type or press, the paper was written on fools-cap by hand, and was often twelve or more pages in length. Both prose and poetry, so called, were contributed by the men. News, real or imaginary, was invited by the editor, who established a box for "correspondence." The paper was read by all the men, and then *The Growler* was sent on to the Klamath Indian Agency, for the pleasure of the soldiers there. On a few occasions, *The Growler* was sent to Jacksonville, in exchange for copies of *The Oregon Sentinel,* whose editor knew and liked most of the men.

One day Thomas S. Warren brought in an exceptionally good plagiarism of The Last Days of Pompeii. The editor suggested that it be sent to Jacksonville by the military express that was to leave the next morning, saying it would be more appreciated if seen in print, and also at some other place than where it was supposed to have occurred. The results were rather startling!

The newspaper printed the story, under the caption *Tremendous Earthquake at Fort Klamath,* with the signature by order of the Commander. The boys had written "by order of Comstock," stringing out the word and making it so nearly illegible that it was accepted as Commander.

The account was copied extensively over the United States, after the editor had put the story on the wire, and it was cabled to Europe. The account is reprinted in at least one book, *Prairie and Rocky Mountain Adventures of Life in the Far West,* by John C. Van Tramp, published in 1867:

"We have singular, if not serious, news to send by the express just leaving. This morning at daylight, we were startled from sleep by the precipitate shock of an earthquake, immediately followed by the noise of distant thunder. But in a little while quiet reigned; everyone was conversing and laughing heartily over the singular phenomenon, but our countenances soon underwent a serious change, for it began to grow

24

dark; the whole heavens were full of a very black cloud or smoke; the air had a very sulphurous smell, and ashes of a brownish color fell fast as ever I saw it snow. We had to use candles in the mess room. Most of us went in to breakfast, but we had only got fairly into our seats, when horror upon horror! The earth seemed rolling like waves of the ocean. Everyone was thrown to the floor, and regained his feet only to be placed in the same position again. With the rattling of dishes, crashing of window glass, crackling of timbers of the buildings, and the screams of frightened boys, you could not imagine a more perfect chaos. Some of us gained the door, and such a sight as met our gaze!

The tall pines around the fort seemed lashing themselves into fury. The wagons in front of the stable were engaged in pitched battle; horses and cattle lying crouched upon the ground, uttering the most pitiful moans; dogs howling, and the unearthly yells of the Klamath Indians encamped near the fort completed the scene. We imagined we were amid the wreck of matter and the crush of worlds. The sutler's store was thrown about twenty feet from its former position. There were no lives lost, and no serious accidents to anyone; but there were quite a number of bruised shins and skinned noses. No serious damage to any of the buildings, all log or frame houses; but I do not think there is a whole pane of glass left at the post.

There are many speculations as to the cause of this most singular freak of nature, but most of us are of the opinion that a volcano has broken loose near the Klamath Marsh, as a continuous dark volume of smoke is seen ascending in that direction. Some of the soldiers have volunteered to go up and find out if we have a monster vomiting fire near us or not. There was about a half hour between the first and second shocks; the first was only perceptible; the second lasted, as near as can be judged from various opinions, from two to three minutes."

The War Department took cognizance of the matter, and following an inquiry as to the truth of the matter, sent order that the perpetrator be sent to Vancouver Barracks in irons. Private Warren begged the editor not to inform on him, and he did not. It was not until the Company had been mustered out that the author's name was ever revealed. Orson A. Stearns, editor of *The Growler*, and teller of this story, reported that as late as 1914, he received letters from scientific men, asking for details of that earthquake which was a hoax.

In July, 1867, the regular army troops relieved the volunteers at Fort Klamath, and thus ended the first phase of life at that frontier post.

Part II

UNITED STATES ARMY POST

Troop A, 1st United States Cavalry, was a welcome sight as they rode into Fort Klamath that first week in July, 1867, with guidons flying. Commanded by Captain John F. Small, this was one of the 120 cavalry troops sent to police the whole western frontier.

This troop came in by way of Fort Bidwell in northeast California, and was composed of battle-hardened and experienced soldiers. Most of them were veterans of the late war; many of them had taken cuts in rank from their war-time status to remain in the army. Some officers had become enlisted men for various reasons—civilian life seemed dull; jobs were hard to come by; some had returned to find their sweethearts already married; some had the problem of drink; some were ex-Confederates. Now, in their short-jacketed blues, fatigue caps pulled low against the sun, and the light gleaming on their insignia of crossed sabres and the brass eagle buttons, boots gleaming and spurs jingling, they had come to garrison Fort Klamath.

Their carbines were laid by, and knapsacks and blanket rolls and canteens unpacked. Heavy McClellan saddles were removed and the horses curried in the big cavalry stables. The troop was assisted by Company I, 1st Oregon Volunteer Infantry, glad to know that it was to be released at last.

So this isolated post became home base for Troop A, 1st Cavalry. They had many a scouting trip against hostile Indians; many a reconnaissance to make. Sometimes they joined the expeditions under George Crook against the hostiles, traveling hundreds of miles, and sometimes were wounded. There was always garrison duty, and some long marches to keep them fit. Such distances as 1,147 and 3,000 miles are recorded.

In September, 1869, an officer left the post for Crescent City, California, to conduct a detachment of forty-five privates of Company K, 23rd Infantry, which was to be added to the force. Between them, they built target ranges, and were required to conduct their practice in conformance with Blunt's *Small Arms Regulations*. The target ranges were 100 by 1,000 yards in extent, and were in the southeastern part of the military reservation, with the high ridges as background. The butts for protection of the markers were built above ground; targets for short range revolved on vertical axes. Range for skirmish practice was on a level area between the post and Wood River. As the line of fire crossed the public road, all travel was stopped during skirmish firing.

The story is told about the infantrymen and their large and broad bayonets. The cavalry ridiculed them and inquired their use. When told that the foot-soldiers used the bayonets for digging small trenches in which to gain cover, the answer was raucous laughter. But there followed a challenge by the men of the infantry. Let the cavalry go to the south end of the parade grounds, on their mounts. At the firing of a starter's gun, they were to charge upon the infantrymen who were going to dig in at the other end of the military reservation. To the astonishment of the cavalry, the soldiers had succeeded in digging out a place deep enough before they could reach the spot, though they had their horses at a dead run.

In 1869, David Linn and others, built a boat to go on Crater Lake, for that beauty spot intrigued the soldiers as much then as it does civilians today.

New buildings were constructed, and the 1870 Post Returns listed them as follows:

1. Quarters 31 by 138 feet
2. Kitchens and mess-rooms, two in a building, each 24 by 100 feet
3. Laundresses' quarters, two, each 16 by 61 feet—for four women
4. Five officers' quarters, 40 by 40 feet each
5. Adjutant and quartermaster offices in one building, 40 by 40 feet
6. Hospital 40 by 40 feet. On the north side, two rooms, each 12 by 12 feet, one a kitchen and the other a mess. On the west side each room 14 by 18, one a dispensary and the other a steward's room. On the east side, one room 16 by 28 feet, used for a twelve-bed ward
7. Quartermaster and commissary storehouse in one building, each 18 by 38 feet, built of hewn timbers with a block house at each end for protection and defense
8. Guard house 40 by 40 feet, of six by six sawed timbers
9. Stables for two companies cavalry horses; two rooms for grain storage of 600 bushels, and a loft overhead to hold 300 tons of hay

Of the post, Henry McElderry, post surgeon, reported on October 9, 1872 that ". . . in the nine years this post has been garrisoned, only one death has occurred from disease. That, in 1865, by enteritis, was thought to have been acquired before he came. Fort Klamath is a healthy spot, and could not have a better water supply."

Despite all the activity, it was a lonely outpost, and desertions occurred—sometimes a lone soldier, sometimes two or three who had been sent on detached service. Oftentimes the stories of gold intrigued them, and led to their desertion. Some of them surrendered themselves as deserters, but more often an officer and a detachment of men took off after them. Upon capture, they were consigned to the guardhouse to await court-martial, when enough officers had assembled. If found guilty, the deserter was branded, according to the custom of that day. No longer was the branding done by iron, but now by India ink or gunpowder tattoo. The deserter was branded by a large D on the left hip.

Transportation of supplies was a constant problem because of the isolated location of the post. As some routes were closed by snow in winter, it was necessary to keep at least a six-month supply on hand. Some of the freight routes were:

Wagon road from Reno Station to Ft. Klamath via Ft. Bidwell, 450 miles, open May to December.

Wagon Road from Red Bluff, terminus of Oregon and California railroad, via Ager and Klamath Ferry and Linkville, 340 miles, open all seasons but heavy in three winter months.

Road from Yreka, opened 1871. Yreka to Ward's Ferry on the Klamath River, 25 miles; Ward's to

Brown's on the Klamath River, 25 miles; Brown's to Link River, 20 miles; Link River to Klamath, 31½ miles; and to Fort Klamath, 4½ miles. The round trip on this route could be made in four days.

The best supply route was considered that from Crescent City, where the port was supplied by ship, thence 200 miles by pack trains through wild and rugged country to Jacksonville, and thence to Fort Klamath. The round trip took two or three weeks. Each mule could carry an average of 250 pounds. Such was the constant use of this route that the mules' hooves cut steps on the trail in the mountains. The cost was 6 cents per pound by ship, then 5 cents per pound by pack train to the fort. The trail could be used July to November.

The second best route was from Portland, via The Dalles and the Deschutes River Valley.

Mail came to the post twice a week. At first it came from old Henley on Klamath River; later from Yreka. The post rider left Yreka early Monday morning, thence to Ward's Ferry; to Brown's stop; to Nurse's hotel in Linkville at Link River bridge; and he reached the fort Wednesday afternoon. The next day he began to retrace his route.

Most of the flour for the fort was produced in the Rogue River Valley, and more than 350,000 pounds of oats were needed for the horses when the garrison was at capacity. One thousand cords of soft wood were needed for cooking and heating.

One interesting supply list follows:

lbs.

Pork	14,394	Tea	16,000
Bacon	7,937	Sugar	71,320
Flour	38,777	Salt	92,053
Hard Bread	3,081	Pepper	75,000
Beans	44,959	Candles	77,680
Rice	14,428	Soap	63,100
Coffee	63,842	Vinegar	45,700

Although vinegar was used with salt to polish their brass buttons, as well as for cooking, one is inclined to doubt the need for 45,000 pounds, and to wonder if all the kegs were really filled with vinegar.

Hay was cut right on the vast hay reserves, and the contract price varied from $4 to $5 per ton. More than 600,000 pounds were needed each year.

There were often difficulties with settlers who had come to the area. In 1871, the commander reported that he had thrown a couple of settlers in the guard house for selling liquor to the men and subverting military discipline. He reported that he had destroyed the five gallons of whiskey he had confiscated.

Trouble with the Indians began soon after the treaty was signed in 1864. The Snakes ran off in 1864, and the Modocs by 1865. Although the Modocs had been participants in the Treaty of 1864, they were not content upon the Klamath Reservation. They claimed that blankets and beef and flour were denied them, so they left for their old home grounds. Several times they were returned by persuasion, though the disaffected band under Kientpus, or Captain Jack, was off the reservation more than on it. They did not get along well with the Klamaths, so the Indian Agent gave them a section known today as Modoc Point,

Post Hospital

Horse Stables

Government marker of finished Basalt at Southeast Corner
of Military Reservation. Still standing.

Cavalry Unit Before Barracks

Abandoned Gazebo at Fort Klamath

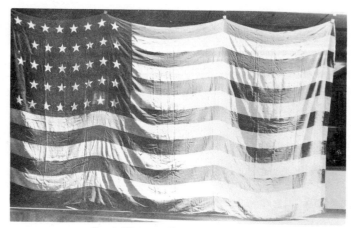

Last Flag to fly over the Post

Guard House

Officer's Duplex

Abandoned Barracks Building

Graves of the Modoc Chiefs, Executed at Fort Klamath

Bringing in the Wounded; Modoc Indian War

Fort Klamath with Flag at Half Staff

Commander's Headquarters

Earliest Fort, built by the Oregon Volunteers

Post Hospital After Abandonment

right on the lake. Despite this, Jack's band was off the reservation in 1870, claiming that the Klamaths molested them and taunted them for living on some-one else's land. So the Modoc band returned to Lost River country, where settlers had already come to stay. These settlers petitioned the Indian Department and the military forces for the removal of the Indians to the reservation. Jack managed to play the whites of northern California against the Oregonians, and used this fact to stall matters, the while demanding a separate reservation. The Modocs who lived up to their treaty provisions were moved to Yainax, in the eastern part of Klamath Reservation.

By 1872, matters were coming to a head. A council was held with Jack at Lost River Gap, but nothing was accomplished, save the more clear revelation of the hostility of the Modocs. Finally, in July of that year, there came an order from the Commissioner of Indian Affairs in Washington to remove Jack's band to the reservation, "peaceably if you can, forcibly if you must." As was so often the case, the soldiers were called upon to take care of some problem which had been bungled by other branches of government. The commander sent out a reconnaissance through the Modoc country to size up the situation.

By November, all peaceful attempts to restore Jack's band to the reservation had failed, and the Indian Agent requested military force to bring back the dissidents. Major John Green, in command of the post, ordered Captain James Jackson, commanding forty men, to go to Jack's camp at the mouth of Lost River and bring back the Indians. They arrived there about daylight on the morning of November 29, 1872. At first, it seemed that Jack and his band would return peacably, but shots were fired, and soon there was chaos. One soldier was killed and several wounded.

While Jackson collected his men and awaited reinforcements, the band of Modocs under Huka Jim sped along the borders of Tule Lake, killing the menfolk of the settler families. Those who had befriended the Indians perished as well as those who had opposed them. This is not the place to tell of the heroism of Mrs. Brotherton and other women; their saga is told elsewhere. Before the slaughter was done, sixteen whites had died. Then Jack's band retreated to the Lava Beds, that rugged area in northern California, just over the Oregon border, interlaced by caves and tunnels of raw lava. This maze of lava, broken and fissured, is an area some ten by fifteen miles in extent. The soldiers learned to call it the roughest place this side of hell. It soon became known as Captain Jack's Stronghold, as indeed it was. General Wheaton was later to say, "I have been twenty-three years on service, the greater part on remote frontiers and generally engaged in operations against the Indians. In this service I have never before encountered an enemy, civilized or savage, occupying a position of such natural strength as the Modoc stronghold." This area, now the Lava Beds National Monument, was at that time bounded on the north by Tule Lake, the source of water for the Indians. The lake extended some forty-five miles in length, mostly in California, so it was necessary for the troops to encircle it in fights with the Modocs. And thus began what was to be the most bitter and sensational of the Indian wars.

It was planned that the military forces would surround the stronghold and present Jack with the choice of surrender or fighting. Colonel Green's and Perry's troops moved, on January 16th, to the high bluff at the southwest corner of Tule Lake. Colonel Bernard was on the east side, with Jackson and twenty Klamath Indian scouts. They were to inch their way forward to get as close as possible without detection. But Bernard, unaccustomed to the land, moved up too close and was attacked by the Modocs, and was forced to retreat. Unfortunately, this disclosed army plans to the Indians. Green, who had never fought Oregon Indians, said that all he needed was howitzers and a snow storm. He had come from fighting Apaches, equipped with only bows and arrows, not Modocs who were often better equipped than the soldiers.

January 17th, 1873, found a heavy fog, but not snow, covering the lava beds. The troops had to inch their way down steep trails to take their planned positions: Mason and the infantry on the extreme left; on the right the howitzers, General Wheaton and staff, and then the volunteers; while on the extreme right was Perry's troop, dismounted. They were supposed to move to the right until they met with Bernard's left, before the Modoc position. But the Modocs, on guard now, opened fire. The fog, instead of being a blessing as the troops had hoped, became a distinct obstacle. They advanced slowly for about a mile and a half; the howitzer was tried, but they feared it might plow into Bernard's troops, so they crept along for another mile or more. About one P. M. the extreme right was brought to a halt by a deep chasm. In the skirmishing and clambering about the rocks, and due to the density of the fog, the volunteers had changed places with Perry's troops and were now on the extreme right. They were pretty well pinned down because of the volleys from Bernard's men which cut down the sagebrush overhead. While

Mason and Green endeavored to make a junction, the troops were encountering a destructive fire as they plunged into a ravine near the lake. Men, crawling over the sharp lava rocks, lacerated hands and feet as well as clothing. Green, when night had fallen, commenced a march of fourteen miles, carrying the wounded in blankets. The troops were demoralized. The wintry season and poor trails had delayed the concentration of troops and supplies; their idea of an easy victory because of superior numbers had failed to materialize; they discovered that the country was favorable to guerilla warfare by the Indians who knew every foot of the country. It is said that when a halt was called, the men fell asleep standing. Their clothing was in shreds, and shoes worn off their feet by the sharp raw lava.

It was past noon of the 18th when they reached Bernard's camp on the east side of the lake. There it was arranged for Jackson and an escort of twenty men to take the wounded to Fort Klamath, seventy miles away, in springless wagons. The gruelling trip took three days before the wounded were in the haven of the hospital. This was such a harrowing experience that Dr. Cabaniss tried a sling between two mules for the wounded. However, this jerky movement added to the pain of the wounded, so Dr. Cabaniss invented his famous mule litter for use in the lava country. He had several made in a Yreka saddlery. The stretcher, fastened on the back of a mule, enabled the soldier to be brought safely to the field hospital in a half-reclining positions that saved him from jolts and dangling limbs.

As evening advanced that 18th of January, the Modocs withdrew, and the stumbling and exhausted men reached camp about midnight. Eleven had been killed and thirty wounded. As one remarked, "Bravery is only pride and good control of your legs that want to run." The dead were left on the field. In this connection, an old Modoc woman, recently deceased at over one hundred years of age, often told how she and other teenage girls were required by Captain Jack to go out after dark and recover what they could from the dead soldiers, especially the "catridges."

Wheaton drilled his men and made his reports, asking for at least three hundred more men, and saying that the chief difficulty had been that they could never see the enemy; that there was nothing more to fire at than a puff of smoke issuing from a crack in the rocks. They got the men all right, but General Canby replaced Wheaton with General Gillem. Two batteries of artillery were ordered from the Presidio at San Francisco by rail, to Redding, then marched via Shasta and Yreka to join Wheaton on the east side of Link River. Howitzers were packed in, in sections, on horseback. From the Department of the Columbia, at Vancouver Barracks, infantrymen were sent by train to Roseburg, the end of the line. They then marched through the winter mud to Ashland; rested a short time and then crawled over the snows of the Cascades on the old Southern Route to Linkville. At once, they marched down to the battle area, weak and exhausted.

About the same time the Modocs were driving out the regulars, the sentimentalists in the East were having their way in Washington. Far away from the real problems, and safe in their seclusion, they sympathized with the poor Indians, unaware of the ruthless suffering inflicted upon the settlers. They urged a "peaceful settlement," and shed many a tear on behalf of the Indians. So, on January 30th, the Secre-

45

tary of War notified General Canby that offensive operations should cease and that the troops be used only to defend citizens or repel attacks. There would be a Peace Commission appointed who would journey to the Modoc country, find the causes of the war and stop it, perhaps, by finding a new place where Jack's band could be located. Everything came to a standstill, for that was orders. Wheaton's plan for boats to carry the howitzers right up to the stronghold was abandoned.

All this delay played right into Jack's hands. He flaunted his new position; kept constantly in touch with all that went on by sending Modoc women on "peace overtures" to the military camp. He now felt safe in his defiance of the government, for he had, of course, defied the government; repudiated his agreements, and had committed murder right on the reservation when he killed an Indian medicine-man. He had been invited to numerous conferences to which he went or not as it suited him, and always with a retinue of fighting men if he went, so it was not surprising that he felt he was the victor in the encounters.

The Jackson County grand jury indicted eight of Jack's band as murderers of settlers, and Governor Grover of Oregon fired off protests that the government was planning to clasp the hands of murderers, but still the peace sentiment persisted, and military men fumed.

In this way weeks passed until the last of March, 1873. Those who knew the Indians feared that they would simply escape to the wilderness when spring came, so troops to the number of 300 were sent to the Tule Lake region. On April 2nd, the Modocs signified their willingness to meet the peace commission on Jack's terms. Though they met with the commissioners, they showed no disposition to accept any but their own ideas, so the truth must be that the Indians outsmarted all of them.

On the morning of the 10th of April, four Modocs visited the headquarters saying that Canby, Gillem, and the commissioners should meet the Modocs in council. They were answered by a written proposition that a general amnesty should be in effect, and a new reservation for Jack should be established. Jack agreed to meet the commission and officers if they would come a mile beyond the council tent. To this, the commission and Canby agreed, though warned by Riddle, the interpreter, and his Modoc wife, Toby, that the Modocs meant treachery. The Riddles entreated the white men to carry arms if they persisted in going. General Canby replied that this would be insulting to the Indians, since they had agreed to come unarmed, so it was that on the 11th he went to his doom.

Canby, Meacham and Thomas of the commission, Dyar, the Indian agent, were accompanied by the interpreters, and they met with Jack and his men, who were armed. Despite all the kind and fatherly words of Canby and the commissioners, upon a given signal from Jack, the Modocs set upon the whites. Jack shot Canby; Boston Charley killed Dr. Thomas, the minister; Schonchin John attacked Meacham. Dyar and Riddle saved their lives by running. Canby and Thomas were dead at once, and Meacham was almost scalped before the Modocs were frightened by word that the soldiers were coming.

The terrible triumph of the Modocs over the soldiers sent to subdue them made news all across the land. A general expression of rage swept the country, at this outcome. It was quite different that a nationally known general and a preacher should be killed—quite different from honest but obscure settlers! Now it was to be war, which soldiers understood, after all the parlaying. Warm Spring Indians were brought in as scouts to replace the unenthusiastic Klamaths. Troops were moved into positions nearer the stronghold.

A general advance was ordered, and fighting continued throughout the day and into the night, under heavy fire from the Modocs. The little Coehorn mortars, with their thirty-inch barrels, lobbed their shells high and they burst within the ragged fissures of the lava tunnels. On the 17th, the final attack on the stronghold was begun. Much to their surprise, they found no Indians there; the Modocs had escaped through some crevice to another position. Their strategy of cutting them off from the lake water had been successful. They did find the remains of an Indian who had evidently tried to chop open a cannon ball which had landed in the caves. During these days, there were thirteen wounded, and one officer and six enlisted men were killed.

Because the military did not know the location of Jack's band, on April 26th, Captain Evan Thomas, commanding five officers and sixty-six men, with fourteen Warm Spring scouts, left Gillem's camp on a reconnaissance of the lava beds to locate the Indians. While eating their lunches, in a flat area surrounded by ridges, Captain Thomas and his men were attacked. They had stacked their arms while they rested, and were entirely unprepared for the attack. Though Captain Thomas and Lieutenant Wright of the infantry were experienced soldiers from the Civil War, these young men were not experienced in Indian fighting. Enfilading rifle fire poured in on them from Black Ridge, a high hill of scoria, extending 400 yards east and west. On the west was a ledge or mass of rocks, with clear spaces intervening. Between the lava and these masses, the ground formed a wide, shallow gulch, with rocks and sagebrush covering it. In front of this large hill was a column of lava, on the top of which was a crater. Indians were hidden in the crater and at the east end. Soldiers were shot down from all directions, and all the time were unable to see their enemies.

Some of the troops fled in panic and disorder. Those who remained were either killed or wounded. Casualties included four officers and two wounded, one dying later; thirteen enlisted men were killed, and sixteen wounded. In army circles, the expressions of regret and chagrin were akin to desperation. Those officers whose lives had been sacrificed were well-known and highly respected. Reporters on the scene were bitter in their comments, saying that no doubt the blame would be passed on and on and admitted by no one. "Killed in a skirmish," said one, "should read killed in a slaughter pen, for that is nearer the truth. This must be called a skirmish, because it was led by a captain, consequently, the dead heroes were killed in a skirmish. For truth and honor's sake let them have the credit justly due them, nor use terms which will indubitably lead to false ideas in the minds of the public." The dead soldiers were buried in a temporary cemetery near the lake shore, while the bodies of the officers were taken to Yreka, where they were put into lead caskets for their trip to San Francisco. "Whipped Again!" shrieked the headlines of the nation's press.

The dead officers were: Captain Evan Thomas, Co. A, 4th Artillery; 1st Lieutenant Thomas F. Wright, Co. E, 12th Infantry; 1st Lieutenant Albian Howe, Co. A, 4th Artillery; and 1st Lieutenant Arthur Cranston, Co. A, 4th Artillery. When their remains were brought in, men grown old and gray in the service of their country wept openly. In many cases it was impossible to recognize the dead because of the Indian mutilations which had defaced the lineaments of their faces. The officers remaining, met and formulated memorial resolutions, in which they quoted Captain Thomas' last words, "I will not retreat a step farther; this is as good a place as any to die." It is good to report that such bravery was not limited to officers alone; for example, one private's body was found crouched by his officer, showing he had tried to shield and save his commander.

One of the poignant stories is that of 2nd Lieutenant George M. Harris, Co. K, 4th Artillery. He and acting surgeon Semig, were the only officers left alive from the Thomas massacre. The surgeon lost a leg, had a paralyzed arm and other wounds which he finally did survive. Young Harris received rifle balls through the lung, back, rib, and flesh wounds, and was in serious condition. When word reached his mother, in Philadelphia, she set out to see her son, if possible before he died. By train to San Francisco she came; then by stagecoach to Redding, thence to the lava beds by mule or horseback or wagon—a mother's love defying all hardships. Young Harris, who had heard she was coming, kept himself alive to see her, and her arrival at his tent was one which caused many a tear on bearded faces. How she ministered to him and stimulated him with her loving words, only a mother would know. His determination and hers that matched, made them know and love each other, but he slipped away in death on the morning of May 12th. He was a graduate of West Point in the class of 1866, and after service in Reconstruction, came West in 1870, as commander of Battery K of his regiment. His men fairly idolized him, and mourned that he should be dead at twenty-five. They often repeated his last words in battle, "Men, we are surrounded. We must fight and die like men and soldiers."

General Jefferson C. Davis relieved Gillem in command, and the war was pushed. There was a skirmish at Scorpion Point on the east side of the lake, between the U. S. troops and Jack's band. The Indians attacked at Dry Lake, where the soldiers charged, routing the Indians. Though there were casualties, this was the first defeat of the Modocs in battle. This defeat caused dissension in Jack's band. Some of them came in voluntarily, and saved their necks by turning against Jack and helping to run him down. On June 4th, Jack himself was captured at the head of Langell Valley, on Willow Creek, near Clear Lake, still wearing Canby's uniform, when one of his men, Steamboat Frank, betrayed him. General Jefferson Davis was about to hang the lot, when word came from the War Department that the Modocs were to be given a regular military trial.

Fort Klamath was alive with activity, for a place must be made in which to house the Modocs during the trial and until their ultimate disposal was decided. Under the supervision of Major Cresson of the 1st Cavalry, Companies E and C of the 12th Infantry constructed a stockade of pine logs in the southwest corner of the post. The stockade was 150 feet long, 50 feet wide, and 11 feet high, and was divided into two sections—one 100 by 50 feet, and the other 50 feet square. The logs were sunk four feet below ground surface, and their bottoms cleated together. The divisions within the stockade were made because the Modocs were at each other's throats, each blaming the other for their capture. The whole was guarded by twenty-four men who stood watch and watch, pacing to and fro along the raised platforms at the stockade corners. No one might enter without permission of the officer of the day, or Modoc pass out except under guard. Rations were issued to the Indians each morning, and they were free to cook as pleased them. They kept inquiring when Jack was to hang, seeming to think that they could then depart at will.

Eleven Modoc murderers occupied the three wooden cells on the ground floor of the post guardhouse, each man in heavy shackles. The cells in which they were confined had gratings for air and light in the rear and a short distance from the ceiling. They were clean and light, but the prisoners could hear little. Their doors opened into the main room of the guard house.

The court martial was begun on July 5, 1873, and the officers were: Colonel Washington L. Elliott, 1st Cavalry; Captain John Mendenhall, 4th Cavalry; Captain Henry C. Hasbrouck, 4th Artillery; Captain Robert Pollock, 21st Infantry and Lieutenant George Kingsbury, 12th Infantry. Major H. P. Curtiss was appointed judge-advocate. Riddle and his wife were hired as interpreters, at $10 per day. Proper legal procedures were carried out, with witnesses for the defense, as well as the prosecution. Jack defended himself by saying that the Klamaths were partly to blame for his deeds, that he had not wanted to fight, and that some of those who helped to perpetrate the murders were escaping death. This was partly true, for, much to the indignation of the citizens, some of the worst Modocs had escaped by turning state's evidence. Only six were tried, and four were found guilty of murder and sentenced to hang; Kientpus (Captain Jack), Schonchin John, Black or Huka Jim, and Boston

Charley. Four scaffolds were erected near the guard house, and there on October 3, 1873, the four Modocs were hanged and their bodies interred just off the post grounds.

It was an event of national interest, and competing newspapers had hired four men, in the hope of being the first to break the news. The four men hired as riders (there was a fine bonus for the man who first reached the telegraph) staked out the routes they thought best, and stationed extra horses along their routes. Ki Matthews, a mulatto, was the winner by minutes. He had chosen the old Rancheria Trail, and made the trip from Fort Klamath to Jacksonville in six hours and forty-five minutes, using three mounts. B. S. Grigsby, born 1863, told how he was in the yard of his father's farm at Eagle Point when Matthews flashed by, quirting his roan at every step, and how he shouted to the boy, "Captain Jack has been hung."

The others of Jack's band were sent to the Quapaw Agency in Indian Territory—thirty-nine men, fifty-four women, and sixty children. They were not allowed to return to the Klamath Country until long after the fort had passed out of existence.

So the Modoc War had ended. Five officers and sixty soldiers had met death; the wounded brought the number to 130. In money, the cost was one-third million, exclusive of pay or equipment. This does not include the lives of hapless settlers and their property.

Fort Klamath returned to a peaceful routine, and the village of Linkville ceased to be the source of dispatches of war—little Linkville, whose publicity had been written in that most potent form of advertising— blood!

The paymaster of the District of the Lakes had a rugged route to take. His territory was comprised of Fort Klamath, Camp Warner and Camp Harney, in Oregon, and Fort Bidwell in extreme northeastern California. Because he carried coin, it was necessary for him to have a military escort at all times. Paper currency was not acceptable right after the Civil War, and if accepted was discounted as depreciated currency, so the officers often wrote to the War Department requesting that their men be paid in coin. It was also on the coin-of-the-realm basis that they hired such civilians as were needed. Considering the fact that so much coin was carried over vast distances, it is really remarkable that none was lost to hold-up men. Often there were streams too high to ford, so rafts were improvised; snow and mud were the principal difficulties. Sometimes the paymaster was able to make less than ten miles a day, and sometimes he was overdue, and a cause for concern. His responsibilities were so great that he rated at least a major's gold leaves.

Mention has been made of the mail carriers. This was found to be a mighty slow method during the Modoc War, so a telegraph line was strung from Fort Klamath, 150 miles to Fort Bidwell, and from Fort Klamath to Ashland, 99 miles distant. This line was built and maintained by the soldiers and operated by the Signal Corps. It was not completed until 1882, and when the fort was abandoned, was sold at public auction.

Many civilians were employed at the post. The sutler, or storekeeper, was the one who furnished the men extras—at a price. As has been mentioned, George Nurse, founder of Linkville which became Klamath Falls, was a sutler at the fort. There was a constant need for the millwright, as much lumber was turned out because of the building in the years following the

Modoc War, and carpenters were frequently hired. The saddler was a busy man, since the cavalry was always on the go. The wages in this period averaged $100 to $110 in coin for most of the artisans. Then there were the contractors who furnished beef, flour, fruit and vegetables. Indians were employed as guides and interpreters, packers, ferrymen and couriers. Their pay, though in coin, was considerably less. No mention is made of the pay for the laundresses, probably since their charges would be made to the individual men.

In 1875 the bones of those who were killed in the Modoc War were brought to the post cemetery, from their temporary burial at Tule Lake. The cemetery at the post was well fenced and the graves marked.

In the post-Modoc War period, the fort was the social center for the region east of the Cascades. Wives and families of the officers lived at the fort, and added a feminine touch to the outpost. At all appropriate times, social events were held there, and they were attended by settlers as far away as Linkville, Langell Valley and Lost River. A little theater was built, and was in almost constant use. The men organized themselves into "The Klamath Minstrels," and gave many performances for the pleasure of their friends. At Linkville, there was organized another group who designated themselves as the "Linkville Amateur Variety Company," and the groups entertained each other. Washington's birthday was one time always celebrated by theatrical performances. "New songs, new dances and roaring farces" were advertised; tickets were fifty cents, and another fifty cents was the price for the dance which followed the theatrical performance.

The big celebration for officers and men of the garrison was that held on the Fourth of July. Salutes were fired at sunrise, noon, and at sunset, from the howitzer battery. Someone, usually the commanding officer, read the Declaration of Independence. Horse, foot, and other races were indulged in during the day, while in the evening, a dramatic performance was given by the thespians. On the Fourth, 1876, for instance, the plays, *Wanted, a Widow,* and *A View in the Dark* were creditably performed. Horse racing was dear to the hearts of the mounted troops, and this was stimulated by the fact that Jay Beach had bought Altamont, a two-year-old, from Colonel West of Georgetown, Kentucky. He became a famous racer and sire. His record of two minutes and twenty-six and three quarters reconds for the mile stood several years. Officers who could, had racers, and many a race was conducted in various communities. The Wood River Valley grass was considered superior for horses—in fact, equal to the famous blue grass of Kentucky. The *Ashland Tidings* once noted that the commander of the post, James Jackson, was a happy man—and why not? He had an attractive young wife and the fastest of the Altamont horses.

Elopements were not infrequent at the post in this time of comparative peace. Some good-looking young soldier at the fort would fall in love with a settler's daughter, or even the daughter of a soldier or officer. If the lovesick swain were turned out of the house by the irate father, an elopement often ensued. The soldier would get leave to attend to personal business; a team would be waiting; the girl would slip out after dark, and they were off to Linkville or Ashland for a wedding. Often these affairs were in the news, sent in by correspondents who showed covert admiration for the elopers.

Sorrow and disbelief were the general feelings one morning in May, 1878, when the body of Lieutenant Harry DeWitt Moore was found in Fort Creek, near the officer's quarters. No signs of violence were found, and it was thought his death was either intentional or that he had perished while under the influence of liquor. A capable and genial officer, he had been very popular. He first joined the army during the Modoc War, just prior to the battle of January 17th, then fresh from West Point. In that battle he had shown great skill and courage. Everyone was glad when the decision was reached that his death was accidental. A single plank was used for a footbridge across Fort Creek. It was decided that he had fallen from it and was strangled by his own scarf as he passed through the flume.

All this time, building was in progress. The old hospital had been found inadequate during the war, so a new one was planned and constructed. It was a two-story frame building, ninety-six by forty-eight feet in size, located at the northeast corner of the parade grounds. It was heated by two stoves, and had ventilators in the floor and roof. A fire bucket and an axe provided protection from that dread happening. In the *Ashland Tidings*, dated July 1, 1876, appeared the following news story: "The new hospital at Fort Klamath is not only an ornament to the Post, but reflects great credit on the architect, builders, and those having supervision of its construction. The only fault is that sickness, where access can be made to this hospital, is too much of a luxury. The post surgeon, Dr. McElderry, has been there for the past five years."

From this post, some fifty of the men went off to

help with the Nez Perce Indian War in May, 1877. When they returned, in November, they had traveled more than 3,000 miles. Captain James Jackson, their commander, who had been breveted Lieutenant Colonel for distinguished gallantry in action and meritorious service in the Modoc War, received the Medal of Honor for distinguished gallantry in action against the Nez Perce, when at Camas Meadows, under heavy fire, he secured the body of a soldier who had been serving under his command in Troop B, 1st Cavalry.

All this time, building was progressing, and finally the post reached its apogee in 1885. At that time the buildings were:

Adjutant's Office, 49 by 33 feet

Officers Quarters, five duplexes, two-storied, 48 by 33 feet

Commissary Office, frame, one story, 40 by 33 feet

Commissary Storehouse, logs, one and a half stories, 20 by 30 feet

Quartermaster Storehouse and Office, frame 80 by 32 feet

Hospital, 2 stories, 96 by 48 feet

Infantry Barracks, frame, two stories, 123 by 23 feet

Cavalry Barracks, frame, two stories, 135 by 33 feet

Old Cavalry Barracks, frame, one story, 320 by 30 feet, now used as school, carpenter shop and ordnance storehouse

Post Stables, frame, 324 by 22 feet

Cavalry Stables, frame, 324 by 22 feet

Hay Shed, frame, 210 by 20 feet. Covers 240,000 pounds of hay

Hay Scales under cover

Granary, frame, 56 by 30 feet. Capacity 350,000 pounds of grain

Cavalry Saddle House, frame, one story, 20 by 20 feet

Wagon Shed, frame, 120 by 20 feet

Blacksmith Shop, frame, 20 by 30 feet

Saddlery, frame, 60 by 20 feet

Laundresses and civilian employees, frame, 60 by 20 feet

Butcher Shop, frame, 15 by 20 feet

Theater, frame, one story, 30 by 60 feet

Old Bakery, frame, one story, 20 by 30 feet

Post Bakery, frame, oven for four companies, 21 by 27½ feet

Hotel, frame, one story, 20 by 49 feet

Laundress quarters, logs, 15 by 20 feet

Wheelwright Shop, frame, 20 by 30 feet

Post trader's Residence, frame, two stories, 20 by 30 feet

Post Trader's Store, frame, one and a half stories, 20 by 30 feet

Post Trader's Stable and Corral, frame

Quartermaster Sergeant's Quarters, frame, one story, 20 by 30 feet

Commissary Sergeant's Quarters, frame, one story, 18 by 20 feet

Oil House, log, one story, 10 by 15 feet

Saw Mill, frame, 30 by 60 feet, needs a good sawyer to put it in shape

Water Tank, frame, supplied by hydraulic ram on Fort Creek

Guard House, log, 32 by 32 feet

Old Stables and sheds, frame, now used as cow and poultry barns

Barber Shop, frame, one story, 15 by 15 feet

Root House, frame, 20 by 20 feet

Magazine, logs, one story, 20 by 20 feet. Double walls, dry and sound

All frame buildings were of fine pine lumber, without knots. The Amusement Room contained a billiard table, card tables, shooting gallery with air guns, fencing foils, boxing gloves, etc. The Post Library contained 438 volumes, magaines and newspapers.

The Post Cemetery, 35 by 45 yards, was 400 yards west of the post.

"Casually at Post" brought such men as these, well-known in the West: Major Robert Williamson, United States Engineers; General George Crook; Brigadier General O. O. Howard; General Irvin McDowell; Major William P. Drum; Major J. C. Breckinridge, and others.

Most of the first surgeons were "contract surgeons," that is, civilians who engaged for a given term. One of these, Dr. Stacy Hemenway, later practiced medicine in the Klamath Country, and was a well-known pioneer.

The first chaplain assigned to Fort Klamath was Charles L. Hequembourg, a Presbyterian minister, in September, 1876.

Officers were sometimes called to other places for court martial duty—to Camp Warner, Fort Bidwell, Fort Vancouver, and even as far away as Alaska. In this situation, the post command was left to a subordinate officer, sometimes for months.

Horses and mules were very important at such an outpost. Sometimes the cavalry purchased horses, but the advertisements showed how strict were their specifications. Horses for the quartermaster must be "dark in color; sound and well-broken; 15 to 16 hands high; five to nine years old; from those submitted, an officer board will select ones suitable." One amusing sidelight is the fact that every horse or mule lost was listed in the Post Returns, telling why it died, and the name of the officer responsible for the horse. Causes of death were listed as: kicked by a mule, colic, inflamation of the bowels, accidentally shot, fell through a bridge and drowned.

One day Captain John Q. Adams sent out a raw recruit, a German, with a team of mules. Soon the recruit was back, crying, "Der mule hav kicked off der cloding; broke de handle of de wagon; and schust runned away mit der self."

Part III

GOODBYE, FORT KLAMATH

The Indian wars were over at last. Reservations had been established and the redmen were located upon them. By 1880, there was talk of saving expense by closing or abandoning as many frontier posts as possible. In 1881, the Secretary of War reduced the Klamath military and hay reserves to 1,000 acres, and released the excess to the Department of the Interior for sale.

At Fort Klamath, military duties included scouting for renegades, white or Indian; building bridges; establishing and maintaining telegraph lines; and the ubiquitous garrison duty. They fenced the post cemetery and repainted the markers for the fifty-nine buried there, among whom were one officer, fifteen soldiers and one civilian from the Modoc War.

At the post, the influence of women was more in evidence, and life was not virorously masculine solely. School for the children was a regular thing, and there was more social life.

However, the professionals had no intention of allowing their men to become soft from easy living. They were sent out on scouts to the east, to Warner and Bidwell, to Sycan Valley and Big Marsh.

In the meantime, there was much correspondence between the President and members of his Cabinet over which posts could be abandoned. This entailed securing the opinions of department commanders; what did the Department of the Pacific think; what about the Department of the Columbia? These commanders, in turn, sought the opinions of those in command at the posts, and thus the wearisome round of military correspondence and indorsements, all done by hand, of course, flowed on.

On May 4, 1886, this document came from the Executive Mansion in Washington, D. C.:

WHEREAS, by the provisions of the first section of an Act of Congress entitled, "An Act to provide for the disposal of abandoned or useless military reservations," approved July 5, 1884, by the President of the United States, whenever, in his opinion, the land inclosed within the limits of any military reservation theretofore or hereafter declared, have become or shall become useless for military purposes, is directed to cause the same or so much of it as he may designate, to be placed under the control of the Secretary of the Interior for disposition, as provided in said Act; and

WHEREAS, the Secretary of War has reported to me, under date of May 1, 1886, that the Military Reservation of Fort Klamath, Oregon, is no longer needed for military purposes, therefore, I, Grover Cleveland, President of the United States, do hereby direct that the said Military Reservation of Fort Klamath, Oregon, being the same as that named in the report of the Secretary of War, hereon before mentioned, be placed under the Secretary of the Interior for disposition as provided for in the same Act of

July 5, 1884, it having, in my opinion, become useless for military purposes.

Given under my hand this fourth day of May, A. D. 1886.

Signed, Grover Cleveland

By the President
William A. Endicott
Secretary of War

What a furor arose when the word reached the Klamath Country! Civilians met in angry mass meetings and fired off petitions, letters, and telegrams to western Congressmen, all protesting the abandonment of Fort Klamath. Reasons given were the still-fresh memories of the Modoc War; the fact that there was friction between the cattlemen and Indian rights to Klamath Marsh, that 100,000 acres of the finest grassland in Oregon; the dangers that might arise, even bloodshed, if the soldiers were removed. Another fact presented was that this was the sole remaining fort in Oregon—Fort Lane, Fort Hoskins, Fort Yamhill, Camp Warner and others having been lost to the state. The Indians were on five large reservations, but who could know when they might go on a rampage? Fort Bidwell, which would then be the nearest military post, was almost 200 miles distant, they said, and before help could be summoned, the settlers might all be killed. Another argument was the fact that many of the buildings were practically new, having been finished only in 1885.

There was also, of course, the fact that the post furnished the means of livelihood for many persons— those who sold meat and flour and vegetables for the garrison; those who were freighters, and those who were the artisans employed at the post.

As for the Indians, some of them, too, had good jobs. One, more frank than most, told an officer, "If soldiers leave, I go to Point of Rocks on the lake, shake my blanket, fire my gun, howl a heap, scare white man and get soldiers ordered back."

When the land had been opened for settlement twenty years before, the rich grasslands had drawn cattlemen.One of these was Fritz Muntz, a German, who had no love for Indians since the Modocs had killed his friend, Wendolin Nuss, first settler, the first day of the Modoc War. Now, living on the edge of the res-ervation, near Bly, he was constantly irritated by the Indians who infringed on his land. One day in the summer of 1886, Indians came looking for wild plums which grew thick on his place. He hated them—one especially. He fired off his gun, over their heads to speed their leaving; but the fourth shot caught the Indian in the neck, killing him. Muntz went to Linkville to give himself up. On preliminary trial he was found guilty of second-degree murder, and his bail was set at $6,000. The more he thought about it, the more nervous he became, since Indians were now wards of Uncle Sam. Eventually he skipped his bond, leaving the new county, named Klamath, with his bail money. It is of passing interest that the bail money was used to build the first courthouse for the new county. This sort of thing could happen again, said the protesters. They also cited the fact that the county had been recently organized, 1882, and was not yet equipped for all the law enforcing elements as yet.

Such was the outpouring of protests, that the Secretary of War wrote to the Secretary of Interior on June 4th that "owing to the large number of petitions against the order, withdrawal of troops had been postponed."

So Company I, 14th Infantry was left at the post, under command of Captain Gilbert S. Carpenter of that company. This was not very satisfactory, for when there was trouble caused by the infringement of cattle owned by whites on Indian lands, it was necessary to call on a cavalry troop from Fort Bidwell, far away. Carpenter was of the opinion that there was no real danger, and that the post could be safely abandoned. Brigadier-General John Gibbon, head of the Department of the Columbia, was rather outspoken when he said, "The Indian Department could handle the matter of cattle intrusion if they really tried. The cavalry did it easily last summer." This was not the opinion of the resident Indian Agent, who said that the Indians were kept under restraint only by force, and he thought the removal of troops imperiled the lives and property of citizens in the entire section of the country.

While all this bickering went on, the men were employed in their usual garrison duties. There was the Hotchkiss mountain rifle and the six-pounder field gun, the field artillery, to clean and polish; Captain George W. Davis of the 14th Infantry needed help in placing three boats on Crater Lake for a survey by the topographical division, who planned a survey of that lake, under Ricksicker.

And so the months passed. On July 20, 1889, the Secretary of War again wrote to the Secretary of the Interior, saying, ". . . the time has come. Please designate an agent from your department as custodian."

On August 9, 1889, Captain Carpenter and staff stood at attention as the great flag of thirty-eight stars was lowered, a sign of abandonment of the post by the military. The captain received the carefully-folded ensign, and moved away. At his command, the garrison moved out; the great freight wagons carrying what had not been buried or left behind. They were enroute to Vancouver Barracks, to which they had been ordered.

Lieutenant William W. McCammon of the 14th Infantry, was left in charge of all public property and of the detachment of men, for a custodian had not yet been appointed. On November 5th the telegraphic communications had ceased, the line having been sold at public auction.

Early in December snow began to fall. The pinfeathers of winter gave a fair indication of the fullfledged bird that was to be the hardest winter known in the Klamath Country. By December 20th, five feet of snow had fallen, and the old cavalry barracks was crushed to earth. McCammon, in all his reports, praised the faithful work done by his detachment, who, despite influenza, managed to save the best of the buildings from being destroyed by the weight of the snow. In February he reported that over 20 feet of snow had fallen, and that only the incessant shoveling done by the enlisted men had saved the buildings. At the same time they had to keep open the trails to wood, water, stables, and to the subsistence stores. They did not lack for food, he said, but it was a struggle to get to the storehouses.

These were the buildings destroyed by the weight of snow: stable; woodsheds and hay shelter; chapel; theater, adjutant's office and the quartermaster storehouse for iron; blacksmith shop; and the balcony of the infantry barracks. He said, in his February report, "The two-story buildings appear to be but one story high, and the one story look like root houses, and even the trees and flag-staff seem strangely diminished in height."

Such devotion to duty as was shown by the men of this detachment surely deserves to be remembered. Their names were: Sgt. Willis E. Morgan, Sgt. John Laipple, Sgt. George W. F. Shirley, Pvt. Charel Andersen, Pvt. Walter H. Green, Pvt. John McCrann, Pvt. John C. Martin, Pvt. John Muering, Pvt. Wilmot C. Williams.

On June 23, 1890, this detachment left Fort Klamath as per their orders. John Loosley had been appointed custodian, and the military men were free to leave. They were on their way to Vancouver Barracks, and the days of Fort Klamath as a military post had come to an end.

The settlers could not forget the old post. Many of them were ex-soldiers who had served at this fort. They remembered all the old days and the pleasures associated with the post. They often gathered for picnics, with the permission of John F. Loosley, the caretaker.

Mr. Loosley had many a tale to tell about the fort. One was that whenever he wanted lead for bullets, he had only to take a container and go to the old rifle range. There he could, in a few minutes, dig out more than enough lead for bullets from the ridge behind the range.

The Fourth of July was always a time for great celebration among the pioneers. Settlers for miles around came to Fort Klamath for the celebration, and Indians joined in the fun, so it was a gala affair. The Indians set up their wickiups, and had a fine time gathering roots and bulbs, for the valley was blue with camas, and the epaws were abundant. They would don their best regalia, feathered bonnets and war paint. They took part in parades and feasting. Later they displayed their dances and gambled far into the night. This continued for many years, until the Indians got the idea that the white men were laughing at them.

Always in the minds of the Oregonians was the hope that Fort Klamath would be re-constituted as a military post, or at least as a training center. As O. C. Applegate wrote to the Secretary of War, the newer buildings were in fine condition, and the soldiers who were stationed there were always happy at that location. Surely this beautiful post, with its empty white buildings, was worthy of a further useful life. It was with this in mind that the Oregon National Guard put on its training maneouvers in 1893. The following account is taken largely from the *Klamath Falls Express,* local newspaper of that time:

"Company D, Oregon National Guard from Ashland, loaded its wagons and brought families with them to the fort; and Troop B Klamath cavalry unit from east of the mountains was on hand to greet them when they arrived. This unit had been organized in 1889 by Captain Siemens, and was praised by oldtime cavalry man James Jackson as one of the most efficient cavalry units in the West. Families arrived in spring wagons and dead-axle wagons, in surreys and on horseback, all laden with their choicest food for the big celebration. Children ran about, and the cool grass felt good to their bare feet; dogs barked; women chattered; and the men in their blue uniforms looked very soldierly as they reminisced about the fort of older days. Captain Siemens was reading the newspaper in the shade of a pine tree. The picture was a pleasing one of patriotic Americans, with Old Glory waving proudly from the flag-staff.

Suddenly there was the clatter of hoofs. A horseman, at full gallop, was seen rounding the west corner of the infantry barracks, a cloud of dust behind him. Gus Melhase, a Wood River settler, without hat or coat, dashed into the midst of the throng, and checking his foam-flecked horse, cried, "For God's sake, where is the commander? The Indians are pillaging our families. They are advancing on the fort. Look at that belt of pines." He pointed to the west, then plied his spurs, to gallop on with his warning. The scene beggared description. Ladies trembled with fright, but brave men rose to the awful emergency. In less time than words can tell, cavalrymen were on their horses; the infantry took the double quick, and military order prevailed.

Captain Siemens gave word to Troop B to charge as skirmishers, and an attack was made on a handful of Indians skulking in the fringe of the woods. A volley was poured from the troop's carbines into the timber, and then a frightful yell was heard. A hundred mounted warriors, led by a white-plumed chief, made an unexpected flanking movement, and broke through the infantry reserve and engaged Oregon's crack cavalry in hand to hand combat. The Indians seemed everywhere, and for a moment brave hearts sank. But not for long. A splendid rally was made by the cavalry, the beautiful guidon in the hands of the sergeant waved courage, and the line of determined men formed to meet the foe. Although superior in numbers, the reds gave way and broke for the timber.

Then a boy on a fleet white pony shot out from the fort. He was Jay Arant, General Compson's orderly. He saluted Captain Siemens, delivered his message, and galloped on. A hollow square was formed by the troop and infantry—and none too soon. A long line of

Indians on fresh horses, and yelling in horrible discord, began encircling the soldiers, at first from a safe distance, and taunting the blue-clads in broken English, began lessening their deadly circle, and the pride of Oregon's soldiers thought their fate might resemble that of Custer's. Colonel James Jackson, whose name graces the pages of the Modoc War, sat grim and silent on his horse. He had heard the first report of Scar-Face Charley's rifle that November 29th, 1872, the initial shot in the bloody tragedy of 20 years previous, and so scenes of blood were not new to him.

The unceasing fire of the soldiers continued, and the savages began to reel in their saddles. The climax was at hand. Suddenly the plumed chief raised his hand for peace, as he rode out from his line. He then lifted his headpiece, and the features of Ivan D. Applegate, scout of three Indian wars and well-known resident of Klamath Country, were disclosed.

What a cheering from the throng! What a flashing of sabres in triumph! What a howling band of Indians who burst into breakneck speed across the valley floor! The Indians and the troopers formed in line again, and officers and chiefs, descending from the saddles, smoked the pipe of peace.

The Great Sham Battle had reached a glorious end, and it was the last event in which the Indians took part. The civilizing influence of church and school and the desire to depart from old customs made them decide not to undertake their war-paint again. After this fray, however, they gathered in the big circus tent, and during the long hours of the night, engaged in their war-dance with tom-tom accompaniment— a final fling, as it were."

All this did not change the mind of the economy-minded Congress, however. Again, in 1900, a movement was put afoot to have Fort Klamath set aside as the "front door" to Crater Lake National Park, and as a recreational area. But before the status of the tract could be ascertained, it was allotted to the Indians, and they began to remove the buildings. The little Williamson Church is made from some of the lumber; in common, unpainted little cabins, one can see such things as graceful and delicate pillars, which were once part of the officers' quarters.

So passed into oblivion that lovely post. The forty white buildings are memories to but a few. The parade ground is a cattleman's pasture, still never having known a plow. The graves of Captain Jack and the others are sunken depressions in the sod. Only the bronze marker, placed near the parade ground by the Eulalona Chapter, Daughters of the American Revolution, marks the area where once stood what was called "the most beautiful frontier post in America"—Fort Klamath.

SOURCE MATERIAL

PRIMARY

The National Archives
Through these departments:
Judge Advocate's Office
Office Chief Engineer
Office Chief Signal Officer
Interior Section, National Resources
Old Army Section
Adjutant General's Office
Abandoned Military Posts
From which were obtained:
The Order to establish this post, March 23, 1863
Historical sketch of the post
Post Returns 1863-1890
Letters sent from the post
Pictures
Cartographic records of locations, surveys, etc.
Plan of fort to scale, showing buildings, creeks, roads, etc.
Microfilms, 800 pages of correspondence, maps, plats, reconnaissances, etc.
House Executive Document No. 122—43rd Congress 1st session
Orson A. Stearns—Memoirs
Correspondence with Robert J. Clark of Missouri, who had been a comrade in Company I, 1st Oregon Volunteer Infantry
United States Military Academy Library
Colonel William H. Powell—*Officers of the United States Army*, New York, 1900
San Francisco Bulletin, 1872-73
San Francisco *Alta Californian*, 1872-73
T. T. Cabaniss—Incidents of the Modoc Campaign,

West Coast Signal, 1877

The *Ashland Tidings,* 1876-89

Klamath Falls Express

Frances Fuller Victor — *Early Indian Wars of Oregon,* Salem, 1894

M. V. Rinehart (ms) Oregon Cavalry, Letters to Mrs. Victor, Brancroft Library, University of California, Berkeley

W. H. Boyle (ms) Personal Observations on Conduct of the Modoc War, Bancroft Library, University of California, Berkeley

Oregon Historical Quarterlies, too numerous to list Department of the Interior

Oregon Pioneer Transactions, most of the issues

San Francisco National Cemetery Records, The The Presidio, San Francisco

Hubert Howe Bancroft, *History of Oregon,* 2 Vol. San Francisco, 1888. *California Inter Pocula,* San Francisco, 1888

The Oregonian, selected issues

Oregon Statesman, selected issues

SECONDARY

Brady, Cyrus T., *Northwest Fights and Fighters,* New York, 1909

Brown, William S., *California Northeast,* Oakland 1951

Carey, Charles H., *History of Oregon,* Chicago 1922

Commissioner of Indian Affairs, *Annual Reports*

Currin, Jeremiah, *Myths of the Modocs,* Boston 1912

Downey, Fairfax D., *Indian Fighting Army,* New York 1941

Sound of the Guns, New York 1955

Dunn, J. P., *Massacres in the Mountains*, New York 1886

Evans, Elwood, *History of the Pacific Northwest*, Portland 1889

Fuller, George W., *History of the Pacific Northwest*, New York 1948

Gatschet, Albert S., *The Klamath Indians of Southwest Oregon*, Washington 1890

Gaston, Joseph, *The Centennial History of Oregon*, Chicago 1912

Good, Rachel Applegate, *History of Klamath County*, Klamath Falls 1941

Harper's Magazine for 1873

Herr, Major General John K. and Wallace, Edward S., *The Story of the United States Cavalry*, Boston 1953

Hodge, Frederick, *Handbook of the American Indians*, Washington 1910

Horner, John, *Oregon, Her History, Great Men, Literature*, Portland 1921

Jacksonville, *Oregon Sentinel*, 1867-68

Klamath Falls, *Herald & News*, many issues

Larsell, O., *The Doctor in Oregon*, Portland 1947

Meacham, Alfred B., *Wigwam and Warpath*, Boston 1875

    Winema and Her People, Hartford 1876

Monroe, Anne Shannon, *Feelin' Fine*, New York 1930

Odeneal, T. B., *The Modoc War*, Portland 1873

Overland Monthly 1873

Payne, Doris Palmer, *Captain Jack, Modoc Renegade*, Portland 1938

Riddle, Jeff C., *Indian History of the Modoc War*, 1914

Ross, John E., *Narrative of an Indian Fighter* (ms), Bancroft Library, University of California, Berkeley

Shaver, F. A., *History of Central Oregon*, Spokane 1905

Sunset Magazine May 1913

Thompson, Colonel William, *Reminiscences of a Pioneer*, San Francisco 1912

Van Tramp, John C., *Prairie and Rocky Mountain Adventures of Life in the Far West*, Columbus 1868

Walling, A. G., *History of Southern Oregon*, Portland 1884

Wilson, Cadet Hugh, Jr., *The Causes and Significance of the Modoc War*, Klamath Falls, 1953

TROOPS ASSOCIATED WITH
FORT KLAMATH

OREGON VOLUNTEERS

First Cavalry
    Troops A, C, F, H, I

First Infantry
    Companies F, I, L

UNITED STATES ARMY

First Cavalry
    Troops A, B, C, D, E, F,
      G, K, L, M

Second Cavalry
    Troops C, I, M

Second Infantry
    Companies F, I

Twelfth Infantry
    Companies A, C, E, G,
      H, K, S

Fourteenth Infantry
    Companies H, K, M

Twenty-first Infantry
    Companies A, C, D, F, G

Twenty-third Infantry
    Companies B, C, D, K

Twenty-fifth Infantry
    Company K

Fourth Artillery
    Light Battery B

Individual officers from Seventh and Eighth Cavalry, and First Second Artillery.

Troop C, *First Oregon Volunteer Cavalry* were the first at the post.

Company I, *First Oregon Volunteer Infantry* were the last of the volunteers there.

Troop A, *First United States Cavalry* were the first federal troops at the post.

Company K, *Fourteenth United States Infantry* garrisoned the post the very last.

IN COMMAND AT FORT KLAMATH

1863 Colonel C. S. Drew, Oregon Volunteer Cavalry
1864 Captain William Kelly, First Oregon Cavalry
1865 Major William V. Rinehart, First Oregon Infantry

1866 Captain Franklin B. Sprague, First Oregon Infantry
1867 1st Lieutenant John F. Small, First U. S. Cavalry
Captain Thomas McGregor, First U. S. Cavalry
1869 1st Lieutenant Greenleaf Goodale, Twenty-third Infantry
1871 Captain James Jackson, First Cavalry
1872 Major George G. Huntt, First Cavalry
Major John Green, First Cavalry
1873 Captain Henry C. Hasbrouck, Fourth Artillery
Lieutenant-Colonel Frank Wheaton, Twenty-first Infantry
1874 Captain James Jackson, First Cavalry
1879 Captain Stephen G. Whipple, First Cavalry
1881 Captain George H. Burton, Twenty-first Infantry
1883 Major E. P. Pearson, Twenty-first Infantry
Captain George H. Burton, Twenty-first Infantry
1884 Captain Leslie Smith, Fourteenth Infantry
1886 Major T. F. Bennett, Second Cavalry
Captain Gilbert S. Carpenter, Fourteenth Infantry
1889 1st Lieutenant William W. McCammon, Fourteenth Infantry

There were often times when the commander was absent from the post, and subordinate officers were in command, sometimes for months.

OFFICERS CONNECTED WITH
FORT KLAMATH—1863-1890

OREGON VOLUNTEERS

Name	Service Connection	First at Fort
Chapman, N. C.	2nd Lt., 1st Cavalry	June 1865
Drew, C. S.	Lt. Col., 1st Cavalry	Aug. 1863, Command
Kelly, William	Capt., 1st Cavalry	Aug. 1863-5, Command
McCall, J. M.	1st Lt., 1st Cavalry	Sept. 1865
McGuire, Patrick	2nd Lt., 1st Cavalry	Aug. 1865
Nobles, John F.	1st Lt., 1st Cavalry	May 1866
Oatman, H. B.	1st Lt., 1st Cavalry	March 1866
Patton, G. C.	2nd Lt., 1st Cavalry	May 1866
Pepoon, Silas	1st Lt., 1st Cavalry	Feb. 1866
Rinehart, W. V.	Maj., 1st Cavalry	Aug. 1865-6, Command
Sprague, Franklin B.	Capt., 1st Infantry	June 1865-7, Command
Underwood, D. C.	1st Lt., 1st Cavalry	May 1864
White, F. B.	1st Lt., 1st Cavalry	Aug. 1863

UNITED STATES ARMY

Name	Service Connection	First at Fort
Adams, John Q.	1st Lt., 1st Cavalry	Aug. 1873
Adams, S. Q.	Capt., Medical Dept.	Jan. 1886
Anderson, Harry	1st Lt., 4th Artillery	June 1873
Anderson, James	1st Lt., 8th Infantry	June 1873
Augur, Colon	Capt., 2nd Cavalry	June 1888
Backus, George B.	1st Lt., 1st Cavalry	March 1880
Bailey, Harry L.	Capt., 1st Cavalry	Nov. 1876
Bendire, Charles	2nd Lt., 23rd Infantry	Sept. 1882
Bennett, Frank T.	Major, 2nd Cavalry	Oct. 1885, Command
Bernard, Reuben F.	Capt., 1st Cavalry	Nov. 1873

OFFICERS (Continued)

Name	Service Connection	First at Fort
Birmingham, Henry P.	Capt. Ass't Surgeon	Sept. 1888
Boutelle, Frazier A.	2nd Lt., 1st Cavalry	June 1871
Breckinridge, J. C.	Major, 1st Cavalry	Sept. 1882, Inspector
Brett, Lloyd M.	1st Lt., 2nd Cavalry	July 1888
Brooke, Edward A.	2nd Lt., 21st Infantry	June 1880
Brown, William H.	2nd Lt., 2nd Cavalry	Oct. 1878
Burke, Daniel W.	Capt., 4th Infantry	March 1888, Inspector
Burton, George H.	Capt., 21st Infantry	June 1880
Callender, John A.	Surgeon	Jan. 1874
Camp, Erskine M.	1st Lt., 12th Infantry	June 1873
Canby, James P.	Major, U. S. A.	1876-1882, Paymaster
Carpenter, Gilbert S.	Capt., 14th Infantry	Oct. 1886, Command
Clarke, William L.	2nd Lt., 23rd Infantry	Nov. 1871
Coe, John N.	Capt., U. S. A.	March 1882, Paymaster
Coxe, Frank M.	Major, U. S. A.	Nov. 1880, Paymaster
Cronkite, Henry M.	Capt. Ass't Surgeon	Oct. 1863
Curtiss, Herbert P.	Major (Judge Adv.)	July 1873
Davis, George W.	Capt., 14th Infantry	July 1886
De Lussy, Isaac C.	Lt. Col., 14th Infantry	Sept. 1889
Dickson, John Muncy	Capt., Ass't Surgeon	Aug. 1877
Douglas, George C.	Surgeon	June 1876
Drum, William P.	Major, 14th Infantry	Aug. 1884, Inspector
Duncan, Joseph W.	1st Lt. 21st Infantry	Dec. 1878
Durant, Henry K.	Surgeon	April 1873
Ebstein, Frederick E.	1st Lt., 21st Infantry	May 1874
Eckels, William H.	Major, U. S. A.	Sept. 1882, Paymaster

81

Name	Service Connection	First at Fort
Edwards, Frank A.	1st Lt., 1st Cavalry	July 1882
Egbert, Augustus A.	1st Lt., 2nd Infantry	Oct. 1884
Eggleston, Virgil S.	Major, U. S. A.	Sept. 1871, Paymaster
Elliott, Washington L.	Colonel, 1st Cavalry	July 1873
Evans, George W.	1st Lt., 21st Infantry	Dec. 1873
Forbes, George L.	Surgeon	March 1880
Fowler, Joshua L.	Capt., 2nd Cavalry	July 1884
Fuller, John E.	Surgeon	July 1873
Fuller, Alfred M.	1st Lt., 2nd Cavalry	Sept. 1889
Fulton, John S.	Surgeon	May 1873
Garvey, Thomas	2nd Lt., 1st Cavalry	April 1879
Gibbon, John	Brig. General, U. S. A.	Sept. 1885, Dept. Com.
Goodale, Greenleaf A.	Bvt. Capt., 23rd Infantry	June 1869 Com. 1871
Goode, G. W.	2nd Lt., 1st Cavalry	Dec. 1881 June 1869,
Granger, Robert S.	Colonel, 21st Infantry	Oct. 1873
Green, John	Major, 1st Cavalry	July 1872, Command
Greene, Frank	Signal Corps	Aug. 1884, Inspector
Grier, Matthew C.	1st Lt., 4th Artillery	June 1873
Gustin, Joseph H.	1st Lt. 14th Infantry	Oct. 1886
Harlow, Frank S.	2nd Lt., 1st Artillery	April 1883
Hasbrouck, Henry C.	Capt., 4th Artillery	June 1873, Command
Hazelton, James B.	1st Lt., 4th Artillery	June 1873
Hemenway, Stacy	Surgeon	Sept. 1876
Henderson, Washington I.	2nd Lt., 1st Cavalry	July 1867
Hequembourg, Charles	Chaplain	Sept. 1873

OFFICERS (Continued)

Name	Service Connection	First at Fort
Hoge, George B.	Capt., 12th Infantry	July 1873
Howard, Oliver O.	Brig. General, U. S. A.	July 1875, Inspection
Hoyle, George S.	2nd Lt., 1st Cavalry	June 1874
Hughes, Robert P.	Lt. Colonel U.S.A.	Sept. 1885, Inspection
Huntt, George G.	Major, 1st Cavalry	Dec. 1871 Command
Jackson, James	Capt., 1st Cavalry	June 1871
Jocelyn, Stephen P.	1st Lt., 21st Infantry	Sept. 1873
Johnston, John L.	1st Lt., 21st Infantry	April 1873
Jones, Roger	Lt. Colonel, U. S. A.	July 1869, Inspector
Jones, William K.	2nd Lt., 14th Infantry	Sept. 1888
Keefer, John B.	Major, U. S. A.	July 1881, Paymaster
Kernan, Francis J.	2nd Lt., 21st Infantry	Nov. 1882
Kingsbury, George W.	2nd Lt., 12th Infantry	June 1873
Knight, G. W.	Surgeon	Aug. 1871
Kyle, John G.	2nd Lt. 1st Cavalry	Jan. 1873
Landis, J. F. Reynolds	2nd Lt., 1st Cavalry	Aug. 1881
LaPoint, Henry C.	1st Lt., 2nd Cavalry	July 1884
Larned, Daniel R.	Major, U. S. A.	1879-1888, Paymaster
Lazelle, Henry M.	Lt. Col., 23rd Infantry	Sept. 1885, Inspector
Lovell, Robert A.	2nd Lt., 14th Infantry	Oct. 1886
Lovering, Leonard A.	1st Lt., 14th Infantry	March 1888
Mason, Edwin C.	Major, 21st Infantry	Oct. 1879, Inspector
McCammon, William W.	1st Lt., 14th Infantry	Sept. 1887, Com. 1889

83

Name	Service Connection	First at Fort
McClernand, Edward J.	1st Lt. 2nd Cavalry	Sept. 1885
McConihe, Samuel	Capt., 14th Infantry	July 1884
McDowell, Irvin	Maj. General, U. S. A.	Aug. 1881, Inspector
McElderry, Henry M.	Capt., Medical Dept.	June 1872
McGregor, Thomas	Capt., 1st Cavalry	July 1867, Com. 1867
Mendenhall, John	Capt. 4th Arillery	July 1873
Merrill, James C.	Capt., Medical Dept.	Aug. 1886
Mesplie, Toussaint	U. S. Chaplain	July 1875
Miles, Nelson A.	Brig. General, Division Commander	Sept. 1889
Miller, James	Capt., 2nd Infantry	Oct. 1884
Moore, Harry DeWitt	1st Lt., 21st Infantry	March 1877
Moss, Henry N.	1st Lt., 1st Cavalry	June 1871
Muhlenberg, John C.	Major, U. S. A.	March 1889, Paymaster
Mulhall, Stephen J.	2nd Lt., 14th Infantry	July 1884
Munday, Benjamin	Capt., Medical Dept.	Feb. 1883
Munn, Curtis E.	Capt., Medical Dept.	Dec. 1887
Nave, Orville J.	Capt., Post Chaplain	Nov. 1882
Nelson, William	Capt., 21st Infantry	Aug. 1872
Otis, Elmer	Major, 1st Cavalry	April 1872, Com. Dist. of Lakes
Park, D. C.	Major, U. S. A.	Feb. 1884, Paymaster
Parke, John S., Jr.	2nd Lt., 21st Infantry	Dec. 1879
Parker, Theophilus	2nd Lt., 8th Infantry	April 1879
Patten, Francis James	2nd Lt., 21st Infantry	Dec. 1881

OFFICERS (Continued)

Name	Service Connection	First at Fort
Pearson, Edward P.	Major, 21st Infantry	Oct. 1882, Command
Perry, David	Capt., 1st Cavalry	April 1872
Pollock, Robert	1st Lt., 2nd Infantry	July 1872, Com. 72-73
Poole, DeWitt C.	Major, U. S. A.	Aug. 1883, Paymaster
Potter, James B. M.	Lt. Col., U. S. A.	1878-79, Paymaster
Potter, Joseph A.	Capt., Chaplain	July 1888
Price, William E.	Surgeon	March 1872
Reagles, James	Surgeon	May 1879
Riley, Thomas F.	Capt., 21st Infantry	Jan. 1879
Robertson, Samuel C.	1st Lt., 1st Cavalry	Nov. 1883
Robinson, Samuel F.	Capt., Medical Dept.	Oct. 1885
Roche, James R.	Major, U. S. A.	1878-81, Paymaster
Roust, W. E.	Ass't Adj. Surgeon	July 1872
Rucker, William A.	Bvt. Colonel	1873, Paymaster
Sargent, Herbert H.	2nd Lt., 2nd Cavalry	July 1884
Schench, Alexander H.	2nd Lt., 2nd Artillery	Oct. 1870
Simpson, John O.	1st Lt., 4th Artillery	Sept. 1873
Skinner, J. D.	Ass't Surgeon	Jan. 1873
Small, John F.	1st Lt., 1st Cavalry	July 1867, Command
Smith, Henry	Quartermaster	Feb. 1885
Smith, Leslie	Lt. Col., 14th Infantry	Aug. 1884, Command
Smith, Rodney	Lt. Col., U. S. A.	1878-84, Paymaster
Sniffen, Culver C.	Major, U. S. A.	1878 Paymaster
Sparrow, Solomon E.	2nd Lt., 21st Infantry	Sept. 1882

Name	Service Connection	First at Fort
Sprague, Charles J.	Major, U. S. A.	1875, Paymaster
Stephens, James	Ass't Surgeon	Jan. 1867
Stirling, F. S.	Surgeon	May 1873
Sully, Alfred	Col., 21st Infantry	March 1874
Sumner, Samuel S.	Major, 8th Cavalry	July 1889, Inspector
wift, Eugene L.	Ass't Surgeon	July 1888
Taylor, Sidney W.	1st Lt., 4th Artillery	June 1873
Thoburn, Stephen C.	2nd Lt., 23rd Infantry	May 1869
Town, Francis L.	Ass't Surgeon	May 1884
Van Voast, James	Capt. 18th Infantry	Oct. 1863, Inspector
Walker, M. M.	Surgeon	Aug. 1887
Wheaton, Frank	Lt. Col., 21st Infantry	July 1873, 1881,
Whipple, Charles	Major, U. S. A.	Paymaster Oct. 1878,
Whipple, Stephen G.	Capt., 1st Cavalry	May 1876
Wilkenson, Melville C.	1st Lt., 3rd Infantry	Sept. 1865
Williamson, Robert S.	Major, U. S. Engineers	Command
Wilson, G. F.	Ass't Surgeon	Sept. 1887 Command
Wingard, Charles W.	Major, U. S. A.	1875, Paymaster
Wittich, Willis	2nd Lt., 21st Infantry	Aug. 1874

CHAPLAINS

1873-4	Charles E. Hequembourg	1183-4	O. T. Nave
1875	Touissant Mesplie	1888	Joseph A. Potter

CITIZEN DOCTORS AT FORT KLAMATH

1863	S. S. Thompson	1879	James Reagles
1864	Henry M. Cronkite	1880	George L. Forbes
1865	W. P. Welch	1880-3	Stacy Hemenway
1866	S. G. Peltz	1883-5	Benjamin Munday
	L. Canning	1884	Francis L. Town
1867	James Stephens	1885	S. F. Robinson
	Lewis Ganung	1886	J. C. Merrill
	Edwin L. Belden		S. Q. Adams
1868	S. E. Holmes	1887	M. M. Walker
1869	George B. Tolman		Curtis E. Munn
1870	C. P. Brierly	1888	Curtis E. Munroe

ARMY SURGEONS

1870	W. B. Cardwell		Eugene L. Swift
1871	G. W. Knight	1888-9	Henry P. Birmingham
1872	William E. Price		
	W. C. Raust		MODOC WAR EXTRAS
1872-6	Henry M. McElderry		Sent at Once to the Field
1873	J. D. Skinner		
1874	John A. Callender		Henry K. Durrant
1876	George C. Douglas		F. S. Stirling
	Stacy Hemenway		John E. Fuller
1877	John Muncy		John S. Fulton
	Dickinson		T. T. Cabaniss

PAYMASTERS

1871-3	Major V. S. Eggleston	1879-80	Major Rodney Smith
1873	Major W. A. Rucker	1879-86	Major D. R. Larned
1875	Major Charles W. Wingard	1880	Major F. M. Coxe
	Major Charles Sprague	1881	Major Charles Whipple
1876	Major R. K. Fowler	1882	Major J. N. Coe
1875-8	Major J. P. Canby		Major W. H. Echels
1877-81	Major J. B. Keefer	1883-7	Major D. C. Poole
1878-9	Major J. B. M. Potter	1884	Major F. C. Park
1878	Major C. C. Sniffen	1886	Lt. Col. Rodney Smith
1878-82	Major James R. Roche	1887-9	Major J. C. Muhlenberg

ARE THERE ROCKS IN CAPTAIN JACK'S GRAVE?

From Modoc War days, there have been rumors that the caskets lowered into the Modoc graves contained rocks for weight, and that those rocks were heard to rattle. The bodies, it was said, were not in the coffins.

On April 19, 1963, the following reply was sent in answer by the Smithsonian Institution:

> In reply to your letter of April 4th, the skull and lower jaw of Captain Jack is indeed part of our collection and is cataloged as USNM 225,070. In the original Army Medical Museum records is a letter from Assistant Surgeon Henry McElderry, U.S.A., stating that he was sending four "heads"—Captain Jack, Schonchin, Black Jim and Boston Charley to the Office of the Surgeon General. These men were stated to have been executed on October 3, 1873, and the heads sent to the Office of the Surgeon General on October 25th of the year. When the Army Medical Museum turned over its skeletal collections to the Smithsonian, the skull and lower jaw were accessioned as part of our collections on January 7, 1904.

INTERESTING BITS ABOUT
FORT KLAMATH

Although the post had been abandoned for more than 70 years, it was necessary to obtain permission of the Judge Advocate to obtain information from the National Archives.

The location of Fort Klamath was at 42 degrees 41 minutes and 34 seconds North Latitude. It was 121 degrees and 59 minutes West Longitude.

Fort Klamath was never moved—yet it stood in four different counties. When it was erected it was in Wasco County. In 1869 it was attached to Jackson County; then Lake County in 1874, and finally Klamath County in 1882.

Interchange of soldiers from Fort Klamath to Arizona Territory was frequently made.

During the Modoc War there were frequent arguments as to whether army style fighting was as effective as volunteer or frontier style. The argument was never settled.

Arms mentioned in the Post Returns:

Needle Guns were issued to citizens during the Modoc War.
Harper's Ferry Rifles
Springfield Rifled Muskets, breech loading
Sharpes Rifles
Spencer Carbines—issued to citizens
Remington Rifles
Henry Rifles

Ammunition:

Fifty-eight caliber mentioned in 1871 report. Goodale said the cartridge boxes, then used for metallic cartridges, held the same number as for the old paper cartridges, viz 40.

Eight thousand rounds of 50 caliber center-primed metallic cartridges were ordered by General Wheaton in 1872; 4,000 rounds of 44 caliber for Remington muzzle-loading revolvers.

Field Artillery at Post:

> Hotchkiss mounted rifle
> Field gun, six-pounder

Swords were ordered, as were great-coat straps. Sabre knots, those heavy-duty doubled leather straps, ending in a leather tassel, were frequently ordered.

The cavalry forage cap had a round, hard, flat top, with a visor on which was the crossed sabre insignia. Cavalry jackets were dark blue, waist length, with brass buttons in eagle design. Officers' buttons had a "C" for cavalry.

A three-day ration was carried by each man because that, plus the arms and ammunition and equipment and rider was all the horse could carry.

A daughter of Captain Carpenter, last in command at the Post, in her later years, recalled some facts about the duplex in which they lived. There was a double living room, separated by sliding doors. Upstairs was a bath, but no running water. This problem was solved by a trap door in the floor, through which the water was lifted from the kitchen in a bucket attached to a rope. The children were bathed in a washtub downstairs. She also recalled the fishing trips to Williamson River; holidays and other gala times when young people gathered from 100 miles around to dance till dawn, and then have breakfast with the soldiers.

In the latter years there was erected on the fort grounds, a little gazebo, built of wood. One can imagine the families gathered around on the grass to hear the music played by the band in this little turreted building at Fort Klamath.